TOP 10 SPORTS ★STARS★

BASEBALL'S TOP 10 PITCHERS

Ken Rappoport

Enslow Publishers, Inc.
40 Industrial Road
Box 398
Berkeley Heights, NJ 07922
USA

http://www.enslow.com

Library of Congress Cataloging-in-Publication Data

Rappoport, Ken.
  Baseball's top 10 pitchers / Ken Rappoport.
    p. cm. — (Top 10 sports stars)
  Includes bibliographical references and index.
  Summary: "A collective biography of the top 10 pitchers, both past and present, which includes accounts of game action, career statistics, and more"—Provided by publisher.
  ISBN 978-0-7660-3466-2
  1. Pitchers (Baseball)—United States—Biography—Juvenile literature. 2. Pitchers (Baseball)—Rating of—United States—Juvenile literature. I. Title.
GV865.A1R35 2010
796.3570922—dc22
[B]

                                  2009027174

Printed in the United States of America

052010 Lake Book Manufacturing, Inc., Melrose Park, IL

10 9 8 7 6 5 4 3 2 1

To Our Readers: We have done our best to make sure all Internet Addresses in this book were active and appropriate when we went to press. However, the author and the publisher have no control over and assume no liability for the material available on those Internet sites or on other Web sites they may link to. Any comments or suggestions can be sent by e-mail to comments@enslow.com or to the address on the back cover.

Illustration Credits: All photos courtesy Associated Press/Wide World Photos, except pp. 5, 18, 21, and 38, courtesy of the Everett Collection, Inc.

Cover Illustration: Associated Press/Wide World Photos.

TOP 10

CONTENTS

Who is Cy Young?

Baseball fans are familiar with the Cy Young Award, given to the best pitcher in each major league every year. Some things not generally known about Denton True "Cy" Young: He threw the first pitch in the first World Series, pitched the first perfect game in modern baseball history, and was the first pitcher in the big leagues to play a consistent starring role in his forties.

Considering that Young bridged the gap famously between the early baseball days and the modern era (starting in 1900), any talk about pitching greats usually starts with him. Young, who recorded an incredible 511 victories, leads the power-packed pitching staff of *Baseball's Top 10 Pitchers*.

Also included are two other pitchers who defied age: Satchel Paige and Warren Spahn.

Like Young, Paige was responsible for a number of "firsts"—including being the first African-American pitcher to appear in a World Series and the first African American to gain entry into the Hall of Fame. Because his arrival in the big leagues was delayed by racial segregation, Paige became the oldest rookie in major league history at the age of forty-two.

Spahn, who won more games than any other left-hander in baseball history, hurled a no-hitter at the age of forty. Before Nolan Ryan completed his record seven no-hitters, no one with the exception of Young had pitched a no-hitter at that age.

The "Top 10" list is not decided on numbers alone. Paige, for instance, helped shape baseball history during a time of integration in the majors. And Sandy Koufax showed the true meaning of courage outside a baseball diamond because of his deep religious convictions.

And where would a Top 10 book be without a relief pitcher, a position that has become more noticeably important over the years? Try Mariano Rivera to represent them all as the top "stopper."

From Young to Rivera, here then are baseball's ten best of the best.

GROVER CLEVELAND ALEXANDER

GROVER CLEVELAND ALEXANDER

The Philadelphia Phillies were in a rush to get out of town. It was the 1916 season. The Phils had just won the opener of a doubleheader in Cincinnati behind ace pitcher Grover Cleveland Alexander.

But there was the matter of playing the second game before making their train. Phillies manager Pat Moran turned to Alexander, his fast-working pitcher. "I'll have to ask you to pitch the second game, too," Moran reluctantly told Alexander. "We've only a little more than an hour to catch the train. Get it over fast, Pete."[1]

"Old Pete," as Alexander was sometimes called, did just that—shutting out the Reds in less than an hour. It was a typical performance by one of baseball's most efficient pitchers.

With one of the best curveballs in baseball, Alexander was a fast worker with pinpoint control. In a career that spanned from 1911 to 1926, he recorded a record 90 shutouts and 373 victories. He won 28 games in his very first season—the best rookie season ever for a pitcher.

From 1911 to 1917, Alexander won 190 games—one-third of his team's total—while pitching in Philadelphia's Baker Bowl, a hitter's ballpark with a right-field wall just 272 feet from home plate. Alexander led the Phillies to their first pennant in 1915.

After the 1917 season, the Phillies sold Alexander to the Chicago Cubs. A draft notice came soon after. Alexander became part of the American fighting forces in World War I.

Returning from the war with shell shock and a partial hearing loss, Alexander also suffered from epilepsy, which causes seizures and an involuntary shaking of the body. Medicines in that day were not effective, and the disease was impossible to control. He tried different measures, including sipping ammonia and drinking alcohol.

Alexander nevertheless won 128 games for the Cubs, even while entering a sanatorium with a drinking problem. He was traded to St. Louis in the midst of the 1926 season. Although his skills had eroded, Alexander—named after a United States president—still had enough left to be a World Series hero at the age of thirty-nine.

It was the 1926 Series. Alexander pitched the Cardinals to a complete-game victory in Game 2, then hurled another complete game in Game 6 to send the Series into a deciding seventh game.

In the seventh inning of Game 7, Alexander was called into the game with the bases loaded and two outs. Alexander looked around to see the three Yankees leading off base and said: "There's no place to put the batter. I reckon I'd better strike him out."[2]

Which he did, on three pitches. Then Alexander pitched two more hitless innings to close out the '26 Series for the Cardinals over a powerful Yankee team that included Babe Ruth and Lou Gehrig.

It was a game and a player to remember for the ages.

ROVER CLEVELAND ALEXANDER

BORN: February 16, 1887, Elba, Nebraska.

· ·

DIED: November 4, 1950, St. Paul, Nebraska.

· ·

PRO CAREER: Philadelphia Phillies, 1911–1917; Chicago Cubs, 1918–1926; St. Louis Cardinals, 1926–1929; Philadelphia Phillies, 1930.

· ·

RECORDS: Won 373 games and pitched 90 shutouts, both National League records. His victory total ranks third on the all-time list.

· ·

LEFTY GROVE

LEFTY
GROVE

Lefty Grove was in a tight spot. The tying run was on third base with nobody out in the ninth inning and the heart of the New York Yankees' batting order coming up: Babe Ruth, Lou Gehrig, and Bob Meusel.

The Philadelphia Athletics' pitcher took a deep breath as Ruth, baseball's home run king, stepped into the batter's box. Just as quickly, Ruth went down on three straight strikes.

Then came Gehrig, the other half of baseball's greatest one-two punch. No problem. Grove set down the "Iron Horse" on three straight strikes.

Finally, the dangerous Meusel stepped in. Grove didn't waste any time, striking out Meusel on three pitches as the A's beat the Yankees 1-0.

Lefty Grove

It was one of Grove's favorite moments in a seventeen-year career. Pitching for the Athletics and Boston Red Sox from 1925–41, Robert Moses Grove led the American League in earned run average nine times, in strikeouts for seven straight years, and in winning percentage five times. The 6-foot-3 southpaw was the anchor of a strong Philadelphia staff that helped the A's win three pennants and two world championships.

Grove hated to lose. He became known for his explosive temper. In 1931, Grove had won 16 straight to tie the American League record. He was going for number 17 against the second-division St. Louis Browns. When a substitute outfielder misjudged a fly ball, allowing a run to score for the Browns, Grove lost a heart-breaking 1–0 game. He was so upset that his temper got the better of him. He tore apart the visitor's clubhouse locker by locker.

But Grove was also known for his integrity and sportsmanship. Although it was common for pitchers to back a hitter off the plate by throwing near his head, Grove refused to do so. "I'd never throw at a man's head," he said.[1]

By 1941, Grove was forty-one years old and needed seven wins to reach 300. By mid-season he had six. "My fastball wasn't so quick anymore, but it was still pretty good," Grove said. "I was throwing a good curve—never heard of a slider and a forkball. The main thing I had was control."[2]

On July 11, he was beaten 2–0. A week later, he lost another one. "My arm still wasn't strong, but I was determined to get that 300, even if I had to do it right-handed," Grove said.[3]

On July 25, it didn't look good for a while. But then the Red Sox took a 10–6 lead into the ninth against the Cleveland Indians. As Grove took the mound, the fans stood and cheered. They continued to cheer with every pitch as Grove put down the Indians one, two, three in the ninth.

Finally, victory. Number 300 was his.

LEFTY GROVE

BORN: March 6, 1900, Lonaconing, Maryland.

· ·

DIED: May 23, 1975, Norwalk, Ohio.

· ·

PRO CAREER: Philadelphia Athletics, 1925–1933; Boston Red Sox, 1934–1941.

· ·

RECORDS: Won 300 games and led the Athletics to two World Series titles. Named the American League's Most Valuable Player in 1931.

· ·

WALTER JOHNSON

WALTER
JOHNSON

The Washington Senators were looking for talent, but when a telegram arrived from their scout, the manager laughed and tossed it aside. "Come out and grab the greatest pitcher in baseball," the telegram said. No one believed it.[1]

Day after day, letters and telegrams from the scout kept arriving at the manager's office. Finally the Senators decided to send someone to check out Walter Johnson. A few days later, a telegram came back: "You can't hit what you can't see."[2]

If not for the persistence of one scout who saw him playing semi-pro ball in Idaho, Johnson might not have been discovered. Famed for a fastball that threw fear into hitters, Johnson was known as the "Big Train" because of the speed of his pitches. He was the strikeout king of baseball while pitching for the Washington Senators from 1907–27.

When he arrived in Washington, Johnson made an immediate impression. Facing the young pitcher in batting practice, the Senators' regulars had a hard time catching up with his fastballs. They threw their bats away in disgust. Johnson started the next day and for years to come.

The kind-hearted Johnson was well aware that his fastball could be lethal. He refused to use a pitcher's greatest weapon—the brush-back pitch. This is a pitch thrown close to the batter to force him back off the plate.

Johnson's pitches were so fast that he feared he could kill a batter if a pitch struck him in the head. Such batters as the great Ty Cobb would take advantage, leaning over the plate knowing that Johnson would go out of his way not to hit him.

Fortunately, Johnson had pinpoint control that made his fastball all the more dangerous. In one season early in his career with the Senators, he walked a total of only 16 batters in 111 innings.

For many years, Johnson was the main gate attraction for the lowly Senators. Drumming up business, Senators owner Clark Griffith called sports editors pleading: "Johnson's pitching tomorrow—give me a headline."

And it worked. Despite the many down years, interest in the Senators remained high.[3]

Despite hurling mostly for sub-par Washington teams, the 6-foot-1, 200-pound right-hander won 417 games, second most in baseball history.

Johnson was at the height of his career from 1913 through 1919. His best year: the 1913 season, when he won 36 games and lost only 7.

WALTER JOHNSON

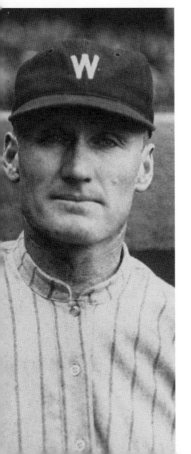

BORN: November 6, 1887, Humboldt, Kansas.

DIED: December 10, 1946, Washington, D.C.

PRO CAREER: Washington Senators, 1907–1927.

RECORDS: Won 417 games, No. 2 all-time on the major league's victory list behind Cy Young. By the time he left the game, he was the all-time leader in strikeouts with 3,509 and once pitched 56 consecutive scoreless innings.

SANDY KOUFAX

SANDY
KOUFAX

It was a momentous decision. Sandy Koufax's teammates were counting on him to pitch. Fans of the Los Angeles Dodgers assumed he would pitch. He was their best hope. So why wouldn't he pitch?

The first game of the 1965 World Series against the Minnesota Twins was scheduled on Yom Kippur, the holiest day of the Jewish calendar year. This day is observed by prayer and fasting. Koufax was Jewish. Ethically and morally, he felt he had to do the right thing. And the right thing was not to play.

This decision made him a hero among those with strong religious beliefs but also brought stinging criticism from others. Don Drysdale started in place of Koufax and lost the game.

Dodgers fans were even more frustrated when Koufax started the second game and only lasted six innings in a 5–1 loss to the Twins. Koufax came back to win Game 5, a 7–0 shutout. The Twins won Game 6 to tie the Series at three games apiece. The Dodgers called on Koufax to pitch Game 7 on only two days' rest.

Koufax had developed an arthritic elbow and pitched in constant pain. At the start of the season, Koufax's elbow was so bad it was questionable whether he'd ever be able to pitch again.

Somehow, Koufax managed to pitch more than 300 innings, set a season strikeout record, and win 26 games to lead the Dodgers from sixth to first in the National League race.

Now it was Game 7. Koufax was having a problem on the mound—no curve ball. Nevertheless, he finished with a three-hitter for his second shutout in four days as the Dodgers beat the Twins 2–0 for the world championship. Koufax's performance earned him the World Series Most Valuable Player award, the second of his career.

Koufax's famous arthritic elbow forced him into an early retirement after the 1966 season with a 165-87 record and 2,396 strikeouts. But for six years, from 1961–66, he dominated baseball as few have done in the game's history. Koufax led the National League in earned run average five straight years, led in wins three times, won three Cy Young Awards, and pitched four no-hitters— the last a perfect game. He was devastating in World

Series play, posting a 0.95 earned run average in helping the Dodgers win three Series.

One of his greatest seasons: 1963, when he won 25 games and lost only 5. New York Yankees catcher Yogi Berra had seen more than he wanted of Koufax after the Dodgers' left-hander struck out a record 15 batters in the opening game of the 1963 World Series against the Yankees.

"I can see how he won twenty-five games," Berra said. "What I don't understand was how he lost five."[1]

SANDY KOUFAX

BORN: December 30, 1935, Brooklyn, New York.

PRO CAREER: Brooklyn/Los Angeles Dodgers, 1955–1966.

RECORDS: Second in career no-hitters with four and one of 17 major league pitchers to hurl a perfect game. Set a major league record, since surpassed by Nolan Ryan, with 382 strikeouts in one season.

CHRISTY MATHEWSON

CHRISTY
MATHEWSON

The crowds came by horse and buggy, on foot and by trolley car. All the men wore suits and bowler hats. Tickets were 75 cents. It was 1905, and the recently established "World's Series," as it was known then, had gripped the attention of America's baseball fans.

The first Series between teams from the National and American leagues had been played in 1903. Now it was two years later, and the New York Giants and their pitching ace, Christy Mathewson, faced the powerful Philadelphia Athletics for the championship.

Mathewson, the darling of the nation's fans, thrilled the crowd with a dazzling performance in Game 1. Batter after batter went down as Mathewson outdueled Philadelphia ace Eddie Plank in the opener for a 3–0 Giants win.

Just three days later, Mathewson was back on the hill for the Giants following a New York loss in Game 2. Down went the A's again as Mathewson fashioned another four-hitter for a 9–0 New York win.

Amazingly, the tireless Mathewson was back on the hill the very next day. He allowed only six hits to complete a 2–0 victory and wrap up the Giants' first championship. More than 100 years later, Mathewson's feat of three shutouts in three World Series starts has never been duplicated. All this happened within a period of six days against one of Connie Mack's greatest teams.

Growing up as the son of a farmer in Factoryville, Pennsylvania, Mathewson was expected to help with the chores. These came first—ahead of his beloved baseball. One day Christy was all set to leave the house for a game, but his mom stopped him. He hadn't finished picking potatoes in the potato patch. Young Mathewson begged his mother to let him go. His friends on the team said, "Please, without Christy, Honesdale will beat Factoryville."

His mother replied, "Factoryville would have to be beaten then."[1]

The next thing she knew, all nine players were out in the patch picking potatoes. Soon they were all picked. Mathewson's mom treated them to a nice lunch, and Factoryville won the game.

Unlike many of the baseball players of his day, Mathewson was a college graduate. At Bucknell, he starred in football and baseball. In 1900, when major league baseball was changing into what is regarded as the modern era, Mathewson was playing professional ball in the minors for $80 a month. The following year, he broke into the major leagues with the Giants.

Mathewson's performance in the 1905 Series was the highlight of a career filled with highlights—including 373 victories. Mathewson led the Giants' staff, helping them win pennants in 1904, 1905, 1911, and 1913.

When the Hall of Fame opened its doors for the first time in 1936, Mathewson was part of the "First Five" along with Babe Ruth, Ty Cobb, Walter Johnson, and Honus Wagner.

CHRISTY MATHEWSON

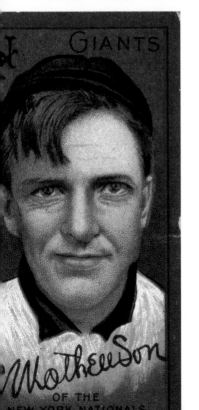

BORN: August 12, 1880, Factoryville, Pennsylvania.

DIED: October 7, 1925, Saranac Lake, New York.

PRO CAREER: New York Giants, 1900–1916; Cincinnati Reds, 1916.

RECORDS: Won 373 games, tied for third place all-time, and had a spectacular career earned run average of 2.13 in his 17 seasons in the majors.

SATCHEL PAIGE

SATCHEL
PAIGE

It was the greatest African-American pitcher against the greatest African-American hitter. At bat was Josh Gibson. On the mound was Satchel Paige, a tall, skinny right-hander with a blazing fastball.

It was the 1942 Negro League World Series. Paige had intentionally walked two batters so that he could confront the legendary Gibson with a World Series game on the line.

After two quick strikes, Paige did the unthinkable: He told Gibson what kind of a pitch he was going to throw—a fastball. Once again, the pitch zipped past Gibson before he could swing. Strike three!

Unfortunately, segregation barred African-American players from the major leagues for many years. So Paige played most of his career in the anonymous Negro Leagues. But he was anything but anonymous.

Nicknamed "Satchel" when he worked at a train station as a baggage handler, Leroy "Satchel" Paige was one of the first African-American superstars in baseball. "Satchel Paige—Guaranteed to Strike Out the First Nine Men." That was how he was sometimes billed. Very often, he did just that.

There were no official records kept in the varied organizations that made up the Negro Leagues. But by his own estimate, Paige won roughly 2,100 games and pitched 300 shutouts and 55 no-hitters in his professional baseball career. Incredible!

He was an entertainer on the mound famed for his colorful antics and his supreme confidence. Every so often, he called in all his outfielders and had them sit around the mound while he struck out the side. Sometimes he would exaggerate his windup, whipping his right arm around like a windmill and lifting his left leg high into the air. His "hesitation" pitch—Paige would stop his windup for a second before throwing the pitch—totally confused most batters.

Paige joined the Cleveland Indians at age forty-two in 1948, one year after Jackie Robinson broke the color barrier in the major leagues. By then Paige had pitched professionally for twenty-two years in all parts of the United States, as well as south of the border. Although he was the oldest rookie in big-league history, as Paige famously said: "Age is a question of mind over matter. If you don't mind, it doesn't matter."[1]

Paige became the first African-American player to pitch in the World Series and the first Negro-League player to be enshrined in the Baseball Hall of Fame.

SATCHEL PAIGE

BORN: July 7, 1906, Mobile, Alabama.

· ·

DIED: June 8, 1982, Kansas City, Missouri.

· ·

PRO CAREER: Cleveland Indians, 1948–1949; St. Louis Browns, 1951–1953; Kansas City Athletics, 1965; plus twenty-two years with a variety of teams in the Negro Leagues.

· ·

RECORDS: During twenty-two years in the Negro Leagues, Paige by his own account pitched in roughly 2,100 games and hurled 300 shutouts and 55 no-hitters.

· ·

MARIANO RIVERA

MARIANO
RIVERA

It was the ninth inning of Game 4 of the 1999 World Series. The New York Yankees were on the verge of sweeping the Atlanta Braves. Mariano Rivera was on the mound for the Yankees. He needed to get just two more outs to end the Series.

It was beginning to look like a comedy skit. Ryan Klesko, the Braves' batter, fouled off a pitch and his bat broke. He trudged off to the dugout to get another. Another pitch, another splintered bat. Frustrated, the batter went back to the dugout for a third bat. This time, Rivera's pitch completely shattered Klesko's bat. He was left with little more than the broken handle as he began running to first on a groundout.

Rivera finished the Series by getting the next batter on a fly ball to left. But it was Rivera's bat-breaking show one out earlier that stood out in everyone's mind. Rivera had developed a powerful weapon to go along with his other fastballs—a pitch called the "cutter." The 95-mile-per-hour fastball broke sharply at the last second. It dipped down and away from right-handed batters and down and in to left-handed hitters. It was considered an unhittable pitch.

Since taking over the role of closer for the Yankees in 1997, the player known as "Mo" to his teammates has been amazingly consistent in a position known for its instability.

The closer is a key position. He usually appears in a game in the ninth inning and only when his team is leading by one or two runs. His job is to preserve the small margin and record a "save." Nobody does it better than Rivera, particularly when it comes to the postseason.

He reached the top of his career when he won the Most Valuable Player award in the 1999 World Series. It was one of four titles in a five-year period that he helped bring to New York.

Because of his deep religious beliefs, philosophy, and supreme confidence, he has been able to withstand the great pressures of his job. He believes everything in life has a purpose—even failure.

In Game 7 of the 2001 World Series, he was unable to deliver a fourth straight title for the Yankees. He felt better when he learned if the Yankees had won, Arizona's

Enrique Wilson would have flown home on an airplane that subsequently crashed. Rivera had lost a game but kept a friend.

Whenever Rivera comes into a game at Yankee Stadium, Metallica's "Enter Sandman" blasts over the loudspeaker. The message is clear: The Yankees' closer is expected to put batters to "sleep" and end the game in a hurry.

MARIANO RIVERA

BORN: November 29, 1969, Panama City, Panama

PRO CAREER: New York Yankees, 1995–present.

RECORDS: One of the greatest post-season closers in major league history, Rivera received the World Series Most Valuable Player award in 1999 and American League Championship Series MVP award in 2003.

NOLAN RYAN

NOLAN
RYAN

Excitement filled the air. Fans lined up in long lines in front of the ticket booths hours before the game. They stood in 101-degree temperatures waiting to see if history would be made. Would this be the night for Nolan Ryan?

The Texas Rangers' right-hander needed just six strikeouts to become the first pitcher in major league history to reach 5,000. The opponents on this hot August night at Arlington Stadium in 1989: the Oakland Athletics.

"When I drove up to the park that night, the attitude of the fans and the electricity in the air was something that overwhelmed me," Ryan said.[1]

The second-largest crowd in Arlington Stadium history watched Ryan go to work:

five strikeouts in the first three innings. No strikeouts in the fourth. Rickey Henderson led off the fifth. He worked the count to three balls and two strikes. He fouled off two pitches—still a full count. Then Ryan fired a 96-miles-per-hour fastball past Henderson.

Number 5,000 for Ryan!

The crowd of 42,869 stood and cheered as Ryan raised his cap in acknowledgment. With the crowd still cheering, Ryan struck out seven more batters for a career total of 5,007.

Henderson didn't mind being the victim of Ryan's milestone strikeout. Quoting other players, Henderson said: "If he ain't struck you out, you ain't nobody."[2]

Ryan's career was all about numbers. Start with the number seven. That's how many no-hitters Ryan pitched in his record twenty-seven seasons with the New York Mets, California Angels, Houston Astros, and Texas Rangers—three more than anyone else.

Another number to consider: 5,714. That's Ryan's record number of career strikeouts—more than 1,000 ahead of runner-up Roger Clemens. (Ryan also struggled with his control throughout his career. He had more walks and wild pitches than anyone in baseball history.)

With his blazing speed, clocked many times over 100 miles an hour, Ryan threw fear into the best of major league hitters. His dazzling speed earned him the nickname of "The Ryan Express." Hall of Famer Reggie Jackson said Ryan was the only pitcher he was ever scared to face. Many players claimed Ryan's fastball had so much movement on it that it "exploded" when it came up to home plate.

Ryan was regarded as one of baseball's greatest all-time "power pitchers." Along with his famous fastball, he also developed a sharp-breaking curve ball that made him unhittable at times.

When he pitched his sixth no-hitter, against the Oakland Athletics in 1990, Ryan at forty-three became the oldest man to do so. Then he broke his own record by no-hitting Toronto at the age of forty-four for No. 7.

Next stop for the "Ryan Express": the Hall of Fame.

NOLAN RYAN

BORN: January 31, 1947, Refugio, Texas.

PRO CAREER: New York Mets, 1968–1971;
California Angels, 1972–1979;
Houston Astros, 1980–1988;
Texas Rangers, 1989–1993.

RECORDS: Pitched seven no-hitters;
baseball's all-time strikeout king with
5,714 strikeouts.

WARREN SPAHN

WARREN SPAHN

What was Warren Spahn's secret? At the age of forty-two, Spahn won a remarkable 23 games for the Milwaukee Braves. He was at the baseball-ancient age of thirty-nine when he pitched a no-hitter against the Philadelphia Phillies.

Now, at the age of forty, he was threatening to do it again.

He stood on the mound looking toward home plate as the hitter stepped into the batter's box. It was April 28, 1961, and the great Milwaukee Braves' pitcher was facing the San Francisco Giants. Three outs to go and Spahn would have his second no-hitter in two years.

Three up, three down—another no-hitter for baseball's famous senior citizen! No one in baseball history had pitched a no-hitter at that age with the exception of Cy Young at the turn of the century.

Over twenty-one major league seasons, Spahn was the most consistent pitcher of his era. He was a 20-game winner, a standard for baseball excellence, in 13 of those seasons and won the earned run average title in *three* different decades.

Spahn was nineteen when discovered by a Boston Braves' scout in 1940. By 1941, the United States was at war. After the 1942 season, Spahn joined the Army. He lost three years of his baseball career but came home a war hero as a winner of the Purple Heart and Bronze Star for bravery. It wasn't until he was twenty-five that he won his first game in the major leagues. Despite losing three years of service in the prime of his career, Spahn recorded 363 victories—the most ever by a left-hander.

Spahn was a control artist, priding himself on out-thinking the hitters and working the corners of the plate. "Hitting is timing, pitching is upsetting timing," Spahn once said.[1]

When most pitchers were slowing down toward the end of their career, Spahn seemed to be speeding up. In 1963, the forty-two-year-old Spahn hooked up with San Francisco's twenty-five-year-old ace, Juan Marichal, in one of baseball's memorable pitching duels.

The Braves and Giants were locked in a scoreless tie after nine innings. The score was still 0–0 in the twelfth. Giants manager Alvin Dark wanted to take Marichal out several times—in the ninth, tenth, and fifteenth innings. Marichal later recalled:

"I told Dark in the fifteenth, 'I'm not leaving while that old guy is still on the mound.' "[2]

In the sixteenth, Marichal was still in there. So was Spahn. The score was 0–0 when the Giants' Willie Mays finally ended the game with a home run off Spahn's screwball.

Even in defeat, Spahn had pitched one of the greatest games of his career—proving he was still at the top of his game at age forty-two. He was on his way to the Hall of Fame.

WARREN SPAHN

BORN: April 23, 1921, Buffalo, New York.

DIED: November 24, 2003, Broken Arrow, Oklahoma.

PRO CAREER: Boston/Milwaukee Braves, 1942, 1946–64; New York Mets, 1965; San Francisco Giants, 1965.

RECORDS: Won more games than any other major league left-hander (363) and was the fifth-winningest pitcher of all time. Appeared in 14 All-star games, most by any pitcher in the 20th century.

CY YOUNG

CY YOUNG

It was a new league and a new start for Cy Young. The year was 1901. Young, a longtime star pitcher in the National League, was coming off his worst season. Some thought the thirty-four-year-old right-hander was at the end of his career.

The National League had been dominant in baseball for many years, fighting off competition in the 1890s to reign supreme as baseball's only major league. Young would be taking a big chance, if he went from the established league to the upstart American League.

Young was determined to prove his critics wrong. He was also lured by the money: a salary of $3,500. Young, who was only making $2,400 with St. Louis, didn't have to think too long.

He made the jump to the Boston Americans, who in later years became the Red Sox. His arrival in Boston gave the new league instant credibility. In his first season in Boston, Young proved himself by leading the league in wins, strikeouts, and earned run average. Young won two games in the first World Series ever played between the National and American leagues, helping Boston win the title in 1903.

Young's career began with a try-out for a minor league team in Canton, Ohio, in 1890. It was Young against the team's star hitter. Young didn't have a uniform, or a catcher.

"I thought I had to show all my stuff," Young said, "and I almost tore the boards off the grandstand with my fastball."[1]

Afterward, the team owner asked the manager, "How's that new kid pitcher?" The manager answered, "Just look at the grandstand."

"It appears as though a cyclone hit it," said the owner.[2]

That's how Denton True Young became known as "Cyclone," later shortened to "Cy." Following a season in the minors, the Cyclone tore through the majors after joining the Cleveland Spiders in 1890. For thirteen of fourteen seasons starting in 1891, Young won no less than 21 games. It was part of his record total of 511 victories.

On May 5, 1904, a baseball game in Boston attracted an unusually large and boisterous crowd for a weekday. The 10,267 fans at the Huntington Avenue Grounds couldn't have asked for a better game. Boston was up 3–0 entering the eighth. Young had not allowed a base runner to that point. He retired the side one-two-three in the eighth, then finished up with three more outs in the ninth. The American League's first perfect game was in the books!

In his following start, Young pitched another six straight hitless innings for a record total of 24 consecutive no-hit innings. When it came to perfection, it was hard to beat Cy Young. In recognition of his greatness, the Cy Young Award is given to the best pitcher in the American and National leagues each season.

CY YOUNG

BORN: March 29, 1867, Gilmore, Ohio.

DIED: November 4, 1955, Newcomerstown, Ohio.

PRO CAREER: Cleveland Spiders, 1890–1898; St. Louis Perfectos, 1899–1900; Boston Americans/Red Sox, 1901–1908; Cleveland Naps, 1909–1911; Boston Rustlers, 1911.

RECORDS: Number one on the career victory list with 511. Also tops in innings pitched with 7,355, career games started with 815, and complete games with 749.

GROVER CLEVELAND ALEXANDER

1. Arthur Daley, "Alexander the Great," *New York Times*, May 21, 1958, p. 41.
2. Arthur Daley, "More on Alex," *New York Times*, November 7, 1950, p. 47.

LEFTY GROVE

1. Michael Mink, "Lefty Grove Earned His Way Atop Baseball's Mound," *Investor's Business Daily, Inc.*, June 22, 2001, <http://www.accessmylibrary.com/coms2/summary_0286-7345468_ITM> (August 14, 2009).
2. Maury Allen, "A Big Day for Old Man Mose," *Sports Illustrated*, September 30, 1963.
3. Ibid.

WALTER JOHNSON

1. Arthur Daley, "Adding a Second Section to the Big Train," *New York Times*, December 17, 1946, p. 48.
2. Ibid.
3. Bob Ryan, "The Big Train," *Baseball Digest*, August 2000, p. 74.

SANDY KOUFAX

1. Tom Grace, "Gathering of the Immortals," *Daily Star* (Oneonta, N.Y.), July 26, 2008.

CHRISTY MATHEWSON

1. *The Literary Digest*, "Matty's Boyhood," June 6, 1914, <http://www.leaptoad.com/raindelay/matty/boyhood.shtml> (August 14, 2009).

SATCHEL PAIGE

1. *The Official Satchel Paige Biography Page*, n.d., <http://www.satchelpaige.com/bio2.html> (November 11, 2009).

NOLAN RYAN

1. Neil Hohlfeld, "The Strikeouts: A Number to Remember—5,714," *Houston Chronicle*, July 21, 1999, < http://www.chron.com/disp/story.

mpl/special/ryan/300427.html> (August 14, 2009).

2. Associated Press, "Ryan Strikes Out Henderson for 5,000th," August 22, 1989.

WARREN SPAHN

1. Rob Neyer, "Few Measure Up to Spahn," *ESPN.com*, November 24, 2003, <http://sports.espn.go.com/mlb/columns/story?columnist=neyer_rob&id=1670588> (August 14, 2009).

2. Joseph DelGrippo, "A Lengthy Mid-Summer Night Game Won on a Homer by a Future Hall of Famer," *Bleacher Report*, August 10, 2009, <http://waww.bleacherreport.com/articles/233779-a-lengthy-mid-summer-night-game-won-on-a-homer-by-a-future-hall-of-famer> (August 17, 2009).

CY YOUNG

1. Associated Press, "Cy Young is Dead; Famed Pitcher, 88," *New York Times*, November 5, 1955, p. S1.

2. Arthur Daley, "The No. 1 Pitcher," *New York Times*, November 6, 1955, p. S2.

FURTHER READING

Banks, Kerry. *Baseball's Top 100: The Game's Greatest Records*. Vancouver: Greystone Books, 2010.

Buckley, James, Jr., and David Fischer. *Baseball Top 10*. New York: DK Publishing, 2002.

INTERNET ADDRESSES

The Official Site of Major League Baseball
http://www.mlb.com/

The National Baseball Hall of Fame and Museum:
Hall of Famers
http://www.baseballhall.org/hofers